EARTHFORMS

GLACIERS

By Martha London

Consultant: Beth Gambro
Reading Specialist, Yorkville, Illinois

BEARPORT PUBLISHING

Minneapolis, Minnesota

Teaching Tips

Before Reading

- Look at the cover of the book. Discuss the picture and the title.
- Ask readers to brainstorm a list of what they already know about glaciers. What can they expect to see in the book?
- Go on a picture walk, looking through the pictures to discuss vocabulary and make predictions about the text.

During Reading

- Read for purpose. Encourage readers to think about characteristics of glaciers.
- Ask readers to look for the details of the book. How are glaciers made?
- If readers encounter an unknown word, ask them to look at the sounds in the word. Then, ask them to look at the rest of the page. Are there any clues to help them understand?

After Reading

- Encourage readers to pick a buddy and reread the book together.
- Ask readers to name two places where glaciers can be found. Find the pages that tell about these places.
- Ask readers to write or draw something they learned about glaciers.

Credits
Cover and title page, © Foto4440/iStock; 3, © nathanphoto/iStock; 5, © Galyna Andrushko/Shutterstock; 7, © Olga Gudumac/iStock; 8–9, © Maridav/Adobe Stock; 11, © schame87/Adobe Stock; 12–13, © Jing Yang/iStock; 15, © Mendilar/Adobe Stock and © Oleh Svetiukha/iStock; 16–17, © Mary Leibundgut/Creative Commons Attribution-Share Alike 4.0 International; 18, © Robert Harding Video/Shutterstock; 19, © kwiktor/iStock; 21, © nullplus/iStock; 22T, © NPS Photo / David Restivo/Wikimedia Commons; 22M, © Mount Rainier National Park/Creative Commons Attribution 2.0 Generic; 22B, © Alexander Bock/Creative Commons Attribution-Share Alike 4.0 International; 23TL, © Explora_2005/iStock; 23TM, © tomch/iStock; 23TR, © Cn0ra/iStock; 23BL, © Supreecha/Adobe Stock; 23BM, © iiievgeniy/iStock; 23BR, © vichinterlang/iStock.

See BearportPublishing.com for our statement on Generative AI Usage.

Library of Congress Cataloging-in-Publication Data

Names: London, Martha, author.
Title: Glaciers / by Martha London.
Description: Minneapolis, Minnesota : Bearport Publishing Company, [2025] |
Series: Earthforms | Includes bibliographical references and index.
Identifiers: LCCN 2024021057 (print) | LCCN 2024021058 (ebook) | ISBN
9798892326223 (library binding) | ISBN 9798892327022 (paperback) | ISBN
9798892326629 (ebook)
Subjects: LCSH: Glaciers--Juvenile literature.
Classification: LCC GB2403.8 .L66 2025 (print) | LCC GB2403.8 (ebook) |
DDC 551.31/2--dc23/eng/20240507
LC record available at https://lccn.loc.gov/2024021057
LC ebook record available at https://lccn.loc.gov/2024021058

For more information, write to Bearport Publishing, 5357 Penn Avenue South, Minneapolis, MN 55419.

Contents

Great Glaciers

A big block of snow and ice is piled high.

The cold sheet shines in the sun.

Brrr!

Glaciers are great.

What is a glacier?

A glacier is a large sheet of ice.

Some glaciers also have snow and rocks.

Glaciers form in cold places all over the world.

Many are in the **Arctic**.

Others can be found on **mountains**.

It takes many years for a glacier to form.

Snow falls and covers the ground.

Then, more snow falls.

The snow turns into ice.

Glaciers are always changing.

A glacier grows and **shrinks**.

Snow piles up in the winter.

Some melts in the spring.

As a glacier grows, it moves.

New ice on top pushes the ice below.

The glacier moves as the ice **shifts**.

Snow falls
Snow piles up
Ice forms
Ice pushes down and out

Glaciers pick up big rocks when they move.

As they **melt**, glaciers leave the rocks behind.

Glaciers also push into the ground and make **valleys**.

Many plants and animals live around glaciers.

Glaciers melt slowly and add water to rivers.

This helps plants grow.

Fish have more water to swim in.

But glaciers are in trouble.

Earth gets warmer every year.

This makes glaciers melt very fast.

We can save glaciers by keeping Earth cool.

Glacier National Park

Glacier National Park has more than 20 glaciers.

Glaciers in the park helped form valleys and mountains.

Scientists study these glaciers to learn about Earth's history.

The park's glaciers are shrinking as Earth warms up.

Glossary

Arctic the area around the north pole

melt to turn from a solid to a liquid with heat

mountains huge landforms that rise higher than a hill

shifts changes place, position, or direction

shrinks becomes smaller

valleys low areas between hills or mountains

Index

Read More

Miller, Debbie S. *Glaciers Are Alive.* Watertown, MA: Charlesbridge, 2023

West, Oliver and David West. *What on Earth is Climate Change? (What on Earth Is . . .).* New York: Enslow Publishing, 2024.

Learn More Online

1. Go to **FactSurfer.com** or scan the QR code below.
2. Enter "**Earthforms Glaciers**" into the search box.
3. Click on the cover of this book to see a list of websites.

About the Author

Martha London lives in Minnesota. She loves spending time outside.